RECONCILING PRA

"Intentional reconciliatio. ⸻ement is hard work. It is also n̲ ᴋ for all who choose to follow Jesus in his ᴜy of Love. But what does this look like? Outlining the interactions of a cohort of very different students from five seminaries, *Reconciling Practices* shows how it is indeed possible to encounter one another not as opposition or other, but as beloved children of God."

—The Most Rev. Michael B. Curry
Presiding Bishop of The Episcopal Church and Author of
Love is the Way: Holding on to Hope in Troubling Times

"Through an experiential lens this text shares the commitment, pain and surprising trajectory of practicing reconciliation, rooted in Christ, that is the call of every Christian (2 Cor 5:20). As both the church and the world face increasing and polarizing divisions, formation in these practices of reconciliation will be essential. This book offers us a way into that work with honesty and with the hope that remains rooted in the reconciling love of God."

—The Most Rev. Linda Nicholls
Archbishop and Primate of the Anglican Church of Canada

"This is the honest account of a brave project, which under other leadership might have been a facile account of a cosmetic project. Kudos to Robert Heaney and his team for having the courage to invite strangers to the same table and, perhaps even more to the seminarians for being willing to stay there when any other choice would have been easier—a parable and a path for a broken church."

—Garwood P. Anderson, Ph.D.

Dean of Nashotah House and Professor of New Testament

"This book is a testimony to what is possible when people of faith take risks for the sake of pursuing the kind of Christian unity that values each human person. It is a refreshingly honest account of listening to and learning from diverse theological perspectives—and the challenges this listening brings. A must read for anyone wanting to engage more deeply with difference for the good of the Church."

—The Rev. Dr. Gabrielle Thomas

Assistant Professor of Early Christianity and Anglican Studies, Candler School of Theology, Emory University

RECONCILING PRACTICES:

LISTENING, PRAYING, AND WITNESSING IN THE MIDST OF DIVISION

EDITED BY
ROBERT S. HEANEY
JACQUES B. HADLER JR.
and HARTLEY HOBSON WENSING

VTS PRESS
ALEXANDRIA, VA · 2022

VTS PRESS

First Published in the United States by VTS Press,
3737 Seminary Rd. Alexandria, VA 22304.
vts.edu

Reconciling Practices: Listening, Praying, and Witnessing in the Midst of Division / Robert S. Heaney, editor ; Jacques B Hadler Jr., editor ; Hartley Hobson Wensing, editor

ISBN: 979-8-813-76644-2

First Edition

CONTENTS

FOREWORD

The Rt. Rev. Dr. Emma Ineson
Bishop to the Archbishops
of Canterbury and York

This short book somehow manages to be many things all at the same time. It is a book about contested issues and disagreement, of course, particularly on the issue of human sexuality. But it is also a book about formation for ministry, and about the church. Additionally, it is a story, a very good story; a story of something that happened and the difference it made. As a former principal of a theological college in the UK, I have seen first-hand the value of seminarians encountering, in the context of theological education, those with whom they disagree, sometimes profoundly and deeply. Formation for ministry is not, and should not be, an exercise solely in filling heads with knowledge (although reading and study is important). It is not only about training people in certain skills (although pastoral and practical placements are crucial). It is primarily the forming of desires to be more in tune with God and God's Kingdom. As James K.A. Smith speculates: "What if education, including higher education, is not primarily about the absorption of ideas and information, but about the formation of hearts and desires?"[1] The story of this book bears witness to that formation of heart in several ways.

Firstly, it speaks to the purpose of formation: we become more Christ-like, of course, but also we become more human, more the persons God has called and shapes us to be. The journey that the *Reconciling Practices* cohort embarked upon was a risky exploration into the complex and contested realm of what it means to be a human being who lives, loves, and worships God, alongside and in relationship with other human beings who do likewise. I am struck by the way in which the participants encountered each other as people, dearly loved by God, and by how they grew to love each other: "We were not talking about ideas. We were talking about each other" (37). As a disciple of Christ similarly wrestling in my own context of the Church of England with disagreements about what it means to be made in God's image—gay and straight, male and female, catholic, reformed, charismatic, liberal—the story of the *Reconciling Practices* cohort

---

[1] James K.A. Smith *Desiring the Kingdom: Worship, Worldview, and Cultural Formation: Volume 1 of Cultural Liturgies* (Grand Rapids: Baker Academic, 2009), 17.

inspires me to look beyond the label and really see my fellow humans as God sees them.

Secondly, we are reminded that truly encountering each other across divides is often a messy and uncomfortable process. It rarely follows a neat trajectory with a beginning, middle, and end. As Robert Heaney points out: "We are ever beginning in the middle of things" (6). Spoiler alert: this book does not have a "happy ending." The original intention of the conversations to provide material for a contribution to the 2020 Lambeth Conference for bishops from around the Anglican Communion was thwarted by Covid. The participants did not miraculously agree with each other on all issues by the end of their meetings. They could not even share in Eucharist together. But this is illustrative of the pain and provisional nature of reconciling dialogue: "What is clear is that this work remains difficult" (31). One of the most profound contributions of this book is the list of definitions of reconciliation at the end. None of them reaches for quick, easy, and cheap solutions. They are much more about the discomfort and pain of simply staying together; walking, listening, witnessing. As a member of Christ's church, imperfect and wounded, this book inspires me to keep on showing up, despite the pain.

Thirdly, this is a book that engenders the formation of hopefulness. The story of *Reconciling Practices* is hopeful because it looks forward, not back. As Cate says, "Reconciliation is not restoration" (40). The cohort discovered that reconciliation across difference is not going back to how things were, because "a clock turned back was unwise, unlikely, or impossible" (8), but reconciliation is about going forward into a future God has imaged for us and to which we are willing to accept the invitation. *Reconciling Practices* causes me to be hopeful for the Anglican Communion, if the reconciling spirit of these seminarians were to be found in all its people, priests and bishops. As a member of the Lambeth Conference Design Group, it is my hope that the story of this group, and the materials that emerge from it, will provide inspiration to the whole Communion. These ten seminarians have a great deal to teach us. *Reconciling Practices* is a story about one group of people in one time and place, but it is applicable to all Christians who seek that formation through difference that is "from God, who reconciled us to himself through Christ, and has given us the ministry of reconciliation" (2 Cor. 5:18).

ACKNOWLEDGEMENTS

A project of this depth and duration relies on contributions from many people and institutions. The editors wish to extend their gratitude to a number of leaders in the Communion and in theological education. At the outset of the *Reconciling Practices* project, the Secretary General of the Anglican Communion, the Most Rev. Josiah Idowu Fearon, Ph.D., spent time with the cohort and shared his unique perspective and insight on the history and identity of World Anglicanism. Thanks are also due to the Rev. Kathrine Bruce, Ph.D., who chaired the selection committee for seminars at the Lambeth Conference, for her guidance and encouragement.

The following leaders of five theological seminaries supported the project, not least in carefully selecting the students, in faithful encouragement and in hospitality over three years: Garwood P. Anderson, Ph.D., President and Provost, Nashotah House Theological

Seminary; the Rev. Christopher Beeley, Ph.D., Director of the Anglican Episcopal House of Studies, Duke Divinity School; the Very Rev. Andrew McGowan, Ph.D., Dean and President, Berkley Divinity School; the Very Rev. Ian S. Markham, Ph.D., Dean and President, Virginia Theological Seminary; and the Very Rev. Henry L. Thompson III, D.Min., Dean and President, Trinity School for Ministry.

We extend thanks also to the following staff of the Virginia Theological Seminary (VTS) Center for Anglican Communion Studies who provided warm hospitality, expert logistics, and proofreading for the project and this publication: Garrett Ayers, Research Assistant; James Morton, Project Assistant; and Molly O'Brien, Administrative Coordinator. The final steps of this book benefited from the guidance of additional VTS staff and resource people whose expertise in the publication process took us over the finish line. We are particularly grateful to Taryn Habberly, Executive Assistant to the Dean and President, and Christopher Poore, Editor at VTS Press.

INTRODUCTION

Robert S. Heaney, Jacques B. Hadler Jr.,
and Hartley Hobson Wensing

In 2016, Virginia Theological Seminary's Center for Anglican Communion Studies failed to get further grant funding from the Luce Foundation on an international project conceived, in partnership with others, on the notion of reconciliation in relation to practices of dialogue, community, and liturgy. That failure became the seed for other projects including *Reconciling Practices*. Central to this project has been the conviction that conflict is embodied and, thus, reconciliation must be embodied. Theological discourse has real material impact on people's lives. Yet, many seminarians and future leaders of the church study and are formed in contexts where embodied disagreement is avoided. Seminarians can learn of historical and contemporary contestation and division without ever coming face to face with the heirs of such contestation or without ever coming face to face with those who continue to see such contestation as vital to Christian witness.

In *Reconciling Practices* we invited five seminaries to appoint seminarians that would form a cohort divided by recent contestation in the broad Anglican family particularly around the issue of human sexuality. Thus, in 2017, ten seminarians from the Anglican Episcopal House of Studies, Duke Divinity; Berkley Divinity School; Nashotah House; Trinity School for Ministry; and Virginia Theological Seminary met to discern whether or not an exploration of embodied conflict and embodied reconciliation was possible. This would be difficult work. This would mean inviting seminarians to step into a process that was nothing like what most of them had experienced in their seminary education thus far. This would be a process where pain and hurt would surface and where resolution in the form of agreement would be virtually impossible.

We are grateful to the Deans of each of the seminaries for supporting the *Reconciling Practices* cohort. Without the support of each of the seminaries this work would not have been possible. We are grateful, and have been blessed, to walk with the seminarians who made up the cohort. Their courage, testimony, and grace has indeed unveiled the possibilities of an embodied practice of reconciliation. We thank God for their witness.

In five chapters, you will have a sense of the deep work the seminarians entered into over a three-year

period taking as their frame the theme set for the fifteenth Lambeth Conference: walking together, listening together, and witnessing together. In chapter 1,
Robert Heaney sets this work into broader Anglican
context. Jacques Hadler and Heaney, in chapter 2,
identify the methodological approach taken in the facilitation work in the project. Chapter 3, written by the
seminarians, captures something of the process they
went through to begin to understand what it would
mean, in practice, to "walk together." It would mean
mutual witness and deep listening. As Christian formation, listening is always done in the context of scripture and prayer. Chapter 4, therefore, provides an
opportunity for Bible study and liturgy designed by the
cohort in the context of their experiences and the
broader context of a fractured church. The final chapter is a witness to how, after three years, the participants understand reconciliation. Along the way, and in
each chapter, there is opportunity for you, the reader,
to pause, reflect, pray, and imagine how reconciling
practices might be embodied in your life and context.

1.

RECONCILING PRACTICES:

A PROCESS IN FORMATION AMIDST DEEP DISAGREEMENT

Robert S. Heaney

I grew up in Northern Ireland. I grew up in a context of violent struggle. Amidst a range of hopes and fears, two irreconcilable visions of the future, founded on readings and misreadings of the past, reigned. These opposing visions could not be reconciled. They were about competing historiographies, cultural identities, and national sovereignties. Theologies and ecclesiologies seldom resourced hope. If anything, religious and theological discourses supported, justified, and embedded division and added greater clarity to difference. No one growing up in Northern Ireland is going to have naïve notions about reconciliation. Even today, I wonder to what extent there is peace in Northern Ireland and to what extent it is but an interim to the next stage of struggle. I am shaped by a conflict that is, almost by definition, irresolvable. That experience has taught me a range of strategies, healthy and unhealthy, for dealing with dangerous conflict. But, I know, I begin from a place of weakness.

As an Irish Anglican, I was formed in a tradition with problematic and peculiar relationships with the Church of England. Since disestablishment in 1869, and in many ways before that, the Irish contextualizations of Anglicanism have resulted in circumstances of strength and weakness, contestation and conciliation. Given, then, my own personal experience and my context of formation I am very wary of easy processes toward some weak version of "reconciliation." Equally, I am suspicious of "settlement" or "resolution" that is achieved through exercises of power and dominance. In contrast to weak "reconciliation" or a top-down exercise of settlement, an argument can be made that instead of viewing contestation as some sort of theological or institutional dysfunction, it may be considered part of what it means for the church to discern the promptings and leadings of the Holy Spirit.[2] If such a view has even some validity, a distinct reading of the formation and re-formation of the faith emerges that can have practical import for situations of conflict today.

---

[2] See Robert S. Heaney and William S. Sachs, *The Promise of Anglicanism* (London: SCM Press, 2019).

A TRADITION EVER IN FORMATION AND REFORMATION

Disagreement and division are part and parcel of the history of the Christian church. Indeed, for many streams of Christian tradition identity is predicated on contestation and separation. In this, Episcopalian-Anglicans are not distinct. Episcopalian-Anglicans are not distinct in seeking to hold together a range of liturgical expressions, theological convictions, and missional priorities.

The history of Anglicanism includes institutional separation. In the sixteenth century, the Church of England declared itself independent of the Pope. Acts of Supremacy (1534 and 1559) would make the monarch the earthly and supreme governor of the Church of England. Since then, a range of Anglican or Anglican-inspired institutions and traditions have emerged in a variety of contexts that stand distinct or in tenuous relationship with the Henrician and Elizabethan reforming Catholicism of the sixteenth century. By the nineteenth century, not least because of the controversies surrounding the complexities of translation and contextualization in international missionary movements and colonial expansion, international fora and institutions began to emerge that would be foundational for current understandings of Anglicanism and Communion. By the twenty-first century, many Anglicans felt a further moment for reform was reached. For some this reform was not possible without some kind of separation from other Anglican Provinces and from Anglican Instruments of Communion.[3] For others, ongoing reform necessitated ongoing commitment to a communion of all Provinces and Instruments. The *Reconciling Practices* cohort did not take a view on institutional communion or institutional distancing or separation. Each and every one of us, however, was shaped by the contested history of Anglicanism(s).

The contestations of Anglicans, throughout history and in international gatherings, can seem somewhat distinct and distant from the work and witness of a local parish. Even in the rarified atmosphere of theological studies in university and seminary, the work of the Anglican Communion can seem distant to the process of formation and preparation for church leadership. Yet, intercultural theological vision and Christian formation in conversation with diverse expressions of the faith is, in part, what it means be a catholic church and a catholic Christian. Like it or not, we do not get to construct our own personal Jesus and our own personal tradition. We always swim in currents deeper and waters wider than we recognize.

---

[3] For information on the Instruments of Communion see Anglican Communion Office, "Anglican Communion: Instruments of Communion," AnglicanCommunion.org, accessed April 19, 2021, http://www.anglicancommunion.org/structures/instruments-of-communion.aspx.

In the power of the Holy Spirit, we are baptized into strange solidarities that we have not chosen and, maybe, would not have chosen (see Gal. 3:25–29).[4] This, according to the Gospel, is the work of God in Christ (I Cor. 12:12–26). This is a spiritual mystery but one which should not leave us mystified. We are called to discern the work of God in God's world (Mt. 6:2–3),[5] we are called to pray that God's will be done (Jn. 17:6–23), and we are called to be witnesses to the reconciliatory power of God in Christ (2 Cor. 5:17–21). The fifteenth Lambeth Conference sought to summarize God's call on the church as walking together, listening together, and witnessing together.[6] But what does that mean in practice? That would be a question bishops—meeting at Canterbury, England in a conference first planned for the summer of 2020—would seek to answer. It would be work done in the midst of contestation and division, and it would be work done in the full glare of the media spotlight. God, of course, could always interrupt the conference and work in miraculous ways to rebirth a Christian movement with

---

[4] See Rowan Williams, *Being Christian: Baptism, Bible, Eucharist, Prayer* (Grand Rapids: Eerdmans, 2014).

[5] See Vatican II, "Gaudium et Spes: Pastoral Constitution on the Church in the Modern World," Vatican.va, December 7, 1965, https://www.vatican.va/archive/hist_councils/ii_vatican_council/documents/vat-ii_const_19651207_gaudium-et-spes_en.html.

[6] See www.lambethconference.org/; Robert S. Heaney, John Kafwanka K, and Hilda Kabia eds., *God's Church for God's World: A Practical Approach to Partnership in Mission* (New York: Church Publishing, 2020).

renewed clarity and comity. Given the histories of the Anglican Communion, at least since the nineteenth century, it would take deep and powerful divine inter-ruption and intervention to heal the fractures in the tradition.

As the Center for Anglican Communion Studies prepared to celebrate its 20th anniversary with a range of program events, including a visit from the Secretary General of the Anglican Communion and a visit from the Presiding Bishop of The Episcopal Church, we were very aware that the historical and contemporary con-testations of the tradition had an impact on a new gen-eration of seminarians and church leaders. Whether acknowledged or not, seminarians were preparing for ministry in a context where the controversies and con-testations of Anglicanism had local consequences. Just as a Lambeth Conference would not turn back the clock, our *Reconciling Practices* project could not reset the counter or create circumstances where separated sisters and brothers could begin again. We are ever be-ginning in the middle of things. We, as with the Lambeth Conference, would begin in the middle of things. As with other Anglican gatherings or projects—our endeavor would likely not return any who had departed from The Episcopal Church nor would it deliver anyone to, for example, the Global Anglican Future Conference (GAFCON) movement. That was never our aim. Yet, all in this divided and fractured Anglican tradition claim to be heirs of a reconciling gospel, and all claim the importance of walking together, listening together, and witnessing together. All read the same scripture and seek to apply it to daily and institutional life.

> . . . now in Christ Jesus you who once were far off have been brought near by the blood of Christ. For he is our peace; in his flesh he has made both groups into one and has broken down the dividing wall, that is, the hostility between us. He has abolished the law with its commandments and ordinances, so that he might create in himself one new humanity in place of the two, thus making peace, and might reconcile both groups to God in one body through the cross, thus putting to death that hostility through it. So he came and proclaimed peace to you who were far off and peace to those who were near; for through him both of us have access in one Spirit to the Father. So then you are no longer strangers and aliens, but you are citizens with the saints and also members of the household of God, built upon the foundation of the apostles and prophets, with Christ Jesus himself as the cornerstone. In him the whole structure is joined together and grows into a holy temple in the Lord; in whom you also are built together spiritually into a dwelling-place for God. (Eph. 2:13–22)

In light of such powerful Gospel words and in light of the contestations, controversies, and cleavages in the Anglican tradition, what was it we hoped for in the *Reconciling Practices* program? At one level, the aim was clear and simple: engage seminarians on the theme of the Lambeth Conference amidst the fractures and brokenness of the Church in the U.S.A.

As a member of the Lambeth Design Group, I had some insight into the hoped-for outcomes of the conference and some sense of the enormity of the task facing us in the second decade of the twenty-first century. I was particularly interested in how the challenges we faced and the program design for a global gathering might connect with local formation. The bishops of the Communion were being asked to consider what it meant to walk, listen, and witness together. What would it mean for local congregations and local leaders to consider the same? What do walking together, listening together, and witnessing together mean for seminarians in a divided church? Given the history and current realities of a fractured tradition our hopes were realistic (maybe pessimistic), but the task was to discern what *in practice* reconciliation might mean in a situation where an agreed-upon settlement or a clock turned back was unwise, unlikely, or impossible. The subsequent chapters in this book give you a glimpse into what practices of reconciliation might mean in one particular context. It is our hope that as you read and pray your way through this short study you might

be inspired to think about how you can practice reconciliation in your own setting.

As it turned out, the Lambeth Conference would be
interrupted. We were reminded in the most tragic of
ways that no human is sovereign. Our best laid plans
can be undone. We stand humbled in the face of disease and death. Even those nations purported to be
among the most "advanced" can do little to combat the
so-called coronavirus. By the end of 2020, 80 million
people would contract COVID-19. The U.S.A would
lead the world with 17 million cases and 310,00 deaths
due to the virus.[7] In the wake of such catastrophe, the
conference was twice postponed. At the time of writing, it is planned to take place in the summer of 2022.
Our initial plan was that this book would be a resource
to be released at Lambeth 2020 when, we hoped, the
Reconciling Practices cohort would present a seminar to
the bishops. Little did we know that global tragedy
would mean our book would be published prior to the
conference.

RECONCILING PRACTICES AS FORMATION

The chapters in this book will describe how the

---

[7] See "Coronavirus Disease (COVID-19)," World Health
Organization, accessed December 19, 2020, https://www.who.
int/emergencies/diseases/novel-coronavirus-2019.

Reconciling Practices cohort sought to walk together (how might we grow to know each other and journey together during our time at seminary?), listen together (how might we read scripture and worship together?), and witness together (what word can we speak to the Communion and world?). Walking, listening, and witnessing might well describe the call to Christian formation. Certainly, it was our hope that *Reconciling Practices* would be formative for ten seminarians from five different seminaries in the U.S.A.

Reconciling Practices was a process *in formation* at a number of levels. At an obvious level the participants were seminarians and, thus, all in a process of formation. These seminarians were engaged in serious theological study and discernment toward church leadership. It was possible that they were distinct and distant enough from factionalism and politics that they were in a place where fresh insight and practice could emerge and make a life-giving difference not only to their own sense of vocation but to their ministry in congregations. These initial assumptions, of course, could have been hopelessly naïve. Right at the beginning, then, we needed some kind of sense of whether or not those assumptions could be relied upon. In short, some kind of "stress test" was needed at the genesis of this process. For without an honest facing up to the depths of division, we might spend much time tentatively mapping the contours of conflict without getting to the personal, relational, and embodied realities of conflict. If the process was to be about *practice* we needed some way to connect controversial issues, contestations, and decisions to the lived reality of the people in the room. We did not want the point of departure to be dominated by a series of disembodied issues about human nature, scriptural hermeneutics, anthropology, or ethics. To begin to walk together meant we would need a sense of the paths that brought us to this juncture. These paths would be paved by historical and institutional narrative, but they would also be paved by personal story and faith commitment.

Reconciling Practices was launched during a visit by the Secretary General of the Anglican Communion to VTS, and the cohort was afforded an opportunity to spend time with him behind closed doors. Given his knowledge, experience, and position, Archbishop Idowu-Fearon was uniquely placed to present an informed reading of the state of modern Anglicanism. This meeting, along with the reading of a series of statements issued by the parties in conflict, meant everyone had a sense of the broader landscape and roads that had led us to this project we had called *Reconciling Practices*. For some in the room, the report by the Secretary General and the documents they read together were familiar. For others, the report and the documents provoked some sense of shock at the depths of division and the tone of disagreement within and without the Communion. Suffice it to say, the state of the Communion and the broad Anglican family presented in documents and in the Secretary General's remarks gave little comfort to anyone. Even, however, in the midst of such macro-level contestation, it was our desire to humanize and personalize the process and the commitments that Christians hold and decisions that Christians make. Thus, participants had opportunity to hear something of the Secretary General's life story at a public event. Each participant in the cohort was also invited to share their own personal faith journey. For if we were to walk together, we would need some sense of where each was coming from. As was to be expected, this initial sharing was somewhat guarded. Nonetheless, the participants exhibited courage and vulnerability as they put words to their faith journey and words to their walk with the risen Christ. Clearly, the five seminaries had selected people of substance and of depth. Without this early and initial testifying the program would have ended before it began. A final dimension to this initial foundational meeting was to allow participants to have some sense of each other in conflict situations. To get at that, we adapted some exercises from the forum theatre methodology pioneered by Augusto Boal.[8] Participants were invited into conflict scenarios with opportunity to intervene in hopes of resolving conflict. Slowly, and hesitatingly,

---

[8] Augusto Boal, *Games for Actors and Non-Actors*, trans. Adrian Jackson, Second Edition (London and New York: Routledge, 2002).

we were inching forward to what it might mean to walk together.

By the end of this initial meeting, two things were clear to me. First, I could not have oversight of the program, be the host, and act as facilitator. At the suggestion of the Rev. Dr. Allison St. Louis, VTS's director of Field Education, the Rev. Jacques Hadler was approached to act as facilitator going forward. Thankfully, Jacques agreed and the process was to be immeasurably enriched and deepened by his experience and skill (see chapter 2). Second, it was not clear at the end of the initial meeting if everyone would be prepared to enter into the depths and fraughtness of this process. Several participants were unsure about continuing even to a second meeting. Some behind the scenes work had to be done after the first meeting to encourage participants to return. The group did reconvene, and each seminary that began the process remained committed to the process. All but one seminarian got to the end of the three-year process.

The *Reconciling Practices* program was formation because it involved seminarians who had already committed to serious theological studies and a process of experiential learning. It was formation because the possibilities for this process could produce a range of skills and a distinct witness not possible through the standard processes of seminary curricula. In another important sense it was formation because of the methodology we would develop as the process moved beyond this initial meeting. The method itself would be shaped by members of the cohort. What it would mean to practice reconciliation amidst deep and painful division would be discerned by the cohort alone. This book is a glimpse into the process and the testimony of the *Reconciling Practices* cohort 2017-2020.

2.

FACILITATING DIALOGUE
AMIDST DEEP DISAGREEMENT

Jacques B. Hadler Jr.
and Robert S. Heaney

In the fall of 2018 Virginia Theological Seminary's Center for Anglican Communion Studies (CACS) invited Jacques to become a co-facilitator of the *Reconciling Practices* program. The purpose of the program was to explore the possibility of reconciliatory practices in an American Anglican tradition riven by intense differences and division. The seminarians began their seminary journey in 2017 and would graduate in 2020, the year the fifteenth Lambeth Conference was planned to take place.

The original intention was for an annual two-day dialogue to be held at Virginia Theological Seminary (VTS). However, as the dialogue unfolded, the seminarians knew that more time was needed. They received the support of VTS and the other partner institutions and a second middler session took place at Berkley Divinity School and a second final year session took place at Nashotah House. They met, then, for a total of five two-day periods over the three years of seminary.

FACILITATOR ORIENTATION

Any facilitator must first seek orientation from the parties or from the host of the dialogue. In this case, as Jacques was not present for the first session, he needed some orientation to the group and the process of *Reconciling Practices*. The four issues of orientation identified here might also serve as guidelines for other facilitators in situations of dispute and division. For, in our experience, the issues of alienation, purpose, commitment, and agency are key considerations in a range of disputes.

First, what was the degree of alienation between the parties in the dialogue? With these seminarians, the situation of alienation was entered into at the first meeting in a series of documents they read together, in an orientation session with CACS, and in a roundtable conversation with the Secretary General of the Anglican Communion. The presenting issues were schism and sexuality. However, the cohort had only touched the surface. The deeper work of how alienation was experienced by each person in the cohort and how that alienation might be experienced within the cohort was yet to be explored.

Second, what was the stated purpose of the dialogue and what goals were agreed upon or might emerge? The purpose agreed upon by the sponsoring seminaries was to explore practices of reconciliation, and not simply ideas or theologies of reconciliation, and perhaps to present the findings at the Lambeth Conference.

Third, what level of commitment to face-to-face and ongoing meeting was possible for this group? Our experience with facilitation is that it is best for a group to gather multiple times in order for group relation-ships to deepen and some degree of trust to develop. The space between meetings allows for individual re-flection on what has happened and for preparation for the next round. This is "Holy Spirit space" for individ-uals to step into so that they reflect and assess in a much less intensely emotional space.

Fourth, what degree of agency did the participants have? That is to say, how free were the individuals in the cohort to act and speak as themselves, and to what extent did they feel constricted as representatives of a particular constituency or position in the dispute? Processes of dialogue can sometimes be constrained when individuals feel they have a representative role. It was our worry that this dynamic might be at work in this group. However, it became clear as seminarians in formation that the participants met to primarily represent their individual experiences and views. This would shift somewhat as the participants learned they would present a seminar at the Lambeth Conference. At the conference they would be representing not only themselves but each other and the process they had been part of for three years.

THEOLOGICAL COMMITMENTS IN FACILITATION

As a Christian facilitator, Jacques has three theological commitments relating to the nature of the church, the call of faith, and the work of the Holy Spirit.

A key text for a scriptural understanding of the *church* remains 1 Corinthians 12:3–12. Here, Paul writes:

> . . . no one speaking by the Spirit of God ever says 'Let Jesus be cursed!' and no one can say 'Jesus is Lord' except by the Holy Spirit.
>
> Now there are varieties of gifts, but the same Spirit; and there are varieties of services, but the same Lord; and there are varieties of activities, but it is the same God who activates all of them in everyone. To each is given the manifestation of the Spirit for the common good. To one is given through the Spirit the utterance of wisdom, and to another the utterance of knowledge according to the same Spirit, to another faith by the same

Spirit, to another gifts of healing by the one Spirit, to another the working of miracles, to another prophecy, to another the discernment of spirits, to another various kinds of tongues, to another the interpretation of tongues. All these are activated by one and the same Spirit, who allots to each one individually just as the Spirit chooses.

For just as the body is one and has many members, and all the members of the body, though many, are one body, so it is with Christ.

Division does not obliterate the body of Christ. There may be many divisions and denominations but there is one church. Within the body of Christ, all have charisms regardless of denomination, institution, or theological system. Therefore, in a facilitation amidst division, each person is coming from a particular process of formation shaped by a particular charism. Facilitators, then, must always seek to discern the diversity of gifts and voices present in each group. Facilitators will encourage expression of all voices and experiences. This discernment and these testimonies are not simply a means to a just process, though they are of course not less than this, they are a practice of the catholicity set out in 1 Corinthians 12.

The call to *faith* is, according to Jesus, a call to love:

One of the scribes came near and heard them disputing with one another, and seeing that he answered them well, he asked him, "Which commandment is the first of all?" Jesus answered, "The first is, 'Hear, O Israel: the Lord our God, the Lord is one; you shall love the Lord your God with all your heart, and with all your soul, and with all your mind, and with all your strength.' The second is this, 'You shall love your neighbor as yourself.' There is no other commandment greater than these." Then the scribe said to him, "You are right, Teacher; you have truly said that 'he is one, and besides him there is no other;' and 'to love him with all the heart, and with all the understanding, and with all the strength,' and 'to love one's neighbor as oneself,'—this is much more important than all whole burnt-offerings and sacrifices.' When Jesus saw that he answered wisely, he said to him, 'You are not far from the kingdom of God.' (Mk. 12: 28–34)

As God is one, the church of Christ is one. The call of the one God to the whole people of God is toward love. We are called to love God. We are called to love our neighbor. This sums up the vocation of the community of faith.

Parties to a facilitation amidst deep disagreement will have experienced a deficit of love. They will be wounded. They will be wounded because they have been misunderstood. They will be wounded because of the misuse and imbalance of power. They will have misunderstood others. They may have misused their power. It is, then, a delicate and deeply risky venture to ask of them, again, to love and to love God and neighbor amidst a wounded church and world. But facilitators do dare to invite people to this discernment and testimony. The work being done is not simply a matter of mind and a searching after theological coherency. It is to enter into a process that will involve the whole person in a multi-dimensional, and often exhausting, process of listening, discerning, and witnessing. To love God and to love neighbor depends upon the work and witness of the Holy Spirit. Facilitators must always then seek the Spirit's blessing and call on the Spirit to deepen their capacities of discernment and community building. Christian facilitators place their trust in the *Holy Spirit*:

> I have not heard recently of committee business adjourned because those present were still awaiting the arrival of the Spirit of God. I have known projects abandoned for lack of funds, but not for lack of the gifts of the Spirit.[9]

John V. Taylor spoke of the Spirit as the "Go-Between God:"

> . . . the gift of the Go-Between God . . . [is that] . . . he opens my eyes in recognition of some other

---

[9] John V. Taylor, *The Go-Between God: Holy Spirit and the Christian Mission* (Eugene: Wipf and Stock, 2015), 5.

being and generates a current of communication between us, in the same way he can open my awareness towards the reality of myself, my shadow and my light, and give me an empathy towards both. This sudden recognition in a single vision of what is and what might be is . . . the gift [the Spirit] imparts to the prophet. This also is [the Spirit's] act of creation—either in the cosmos or in the self. It begins with the recognition of absolute otherness and goes on to the interplay of communion.[10]

The Spirit is at work within us, at work in the world, at work in the church. But the Holy Spirit is also and always at work in the spaces between. The Spirit is the intermediary. Thus, in facilitation, the spaces for movement, development, and discovery are already spaces where the Spirit is present and at work. Facilitators should not, then, over-program or over-determine any outcomes or method. There should always be the capacity for an "unfolding" of process and surprise in the outcome.

---

10 Taylor, *Go-Between God*, 23.

BEGINNING A FACILITATED PROCESS

In taking the role of facilitator in *Reconciling Practices* conversations, Jacques saw his role as:

(i) Promoting the expression of all voices at the table;

(ii) Listening to each voice at the table, valuing it, and seeking clarification of contributions;

(iii) Creating space for responses to voices at the table;

(iv) Teaching the group the dynamics of dealing with differences and the emotional process of human interactions;

(v) Lowering anxiety. A facilitator must model this even in difficult and emotionally charged conversations.

Processes of dialogue across difference are, by definition, charged with emotion. Anxiety is high. Anxiety takes on a series of forms including: polarization; blaming the other for the perceived problems arising from the difference; defensive or apologetic tones; solidarity with those perceived to belong to one's position and enmity towards those perceived as the enemy; distorted perceptions of the other; guardedness in self-expression; low-risk initial sharing; and avoiding controversial subjects. A facilitator is wise to be clear on their role while always being cognizant of the ways in which anxiety exhibits itself. Given this, a facilitator will seek to promote a calm and safe environment through a centeredness in the Holy Spirit and in non-judgmental and encouraging interactions with each participant.

The *Reconciling Practices* cohort met together for the second time over lunch in what was to be a two-day program. Hospitality is key to facilitation, and each of the institutions in the program were generous in welcome, accommodation, and refreshments. There is always an initial awkwardness when meeting for the first time or reconvening after a time apart. Facilitators have a role in these informal times to be open, welcoming, and non-anxious. In more formal gatherings, and re-gatherings, a clear strategy toward building a culture where the aforementioned practices of facilitation can evoke practices of reconciliation is needed. In our work together principles toward humanization, clarification, a culture of dialogue, and instruction became important.

One's neighbor is a fellow human being and child of God. This is a core commitment that people of faith hold. Yet, inherent in the deepest of conflicts and violence are processes of dehumanization. Both violence and dehumanization are at work in conflict within the body of Christ. In countering this, facilitators will seek to put in place processes of *humanization*. At the beginning of each meeting, Jacques invited each person to share for up to ten minutes. A range of prompts can be used to launch such a process but the aim is always the same: invite each other to recognize the humanity in others and the shared human experience that exists even in the deepest of conflict. In the very first meeting of the cohort, each participant was invited to share their faith journey. In this second meeting, participants were invited to (re)introduce themselves and reflect on their expectations and hopes since the last meeting and for this meeting. In this process, Jacques positioned himself as a participant facilitator, warming the water by opening with the sharing of his person and approach, and then inviting the others to share.

Clarity and ongoing *clarification* on process, aims, what the facilitator is hearing in the conversation, and reflecting back to the group any necessary change in aims or process is important. In this group process, Jacques began with clarifying the purpose of the dialogue with the group along with the goals relevant to each particular two-day meeting. As the process moved forward—and the depths of the emotional and spiritual efforts involved in getting to know one another and the issues that divided the group took its toll—reform of the program was often necessary. Certainly, building in more time for self-reflection and informal times together became important for this group. A facilitated process like this that prizes clarity and is open to redesign only serves to deepen the dialogue. For example, as the group developed deeper relationships, it became clear that members from other seminaries wanted to host the group. This became an important part of *Reconciling Practices* that was not envisioned in the initial design.

Developing a particular *culture* of dialogue with a set of agreed upon norms equips participants with confidence to engage and with expectations around how their engagement will be received. Jacques, thus, invited the cohort to develop communication and relational norms so that each could feel safe in expressing their voice. As a way into this exercise, Jacques decided to share two norms that he had found to be helpful in dialogue. First, do not dominate the conversation either by long-winded monologues or by presenting as an authority on the issue at hand. Second, preserve space. That is to say, give opportunity for even the quietest person in the group and be comfortable with silence within the dialogue. With these two norms written on the board, Jacques invited others to share norms they felt would aid self-expression and trust. After all had a chance to contribute, we looked over the list, where necessary clarified some items, and accepted these as our norms. In each subsequent meeting, these norms were reviewed.

Every facilitator is formed in a particular culture or cultures and trained to approach facilitation on the basis of certain philosophies or assumptions. We felt it important to make such assumptions explicit. Jacques, therefore, not only facilitated conversation but gave *instruction* on a form of facilitation based on Bowen

Family Systems Theory. In this second meeting, Jacques offered about an hour of instruction on some dynamics of anxiety, dealing with differences, and emotional dynamics in groups. He offered this instruction to bring to awareness some emotional forces that might undermine their best functioning in the group interactions. How participants react and act in difficult circumstances is well practiced. Being aware of such dynamics and emotional forces can equip participants to moderate themselves and enter more deeply into dialogue and discernment. It was evident that the group found this useful. Consequently, in each subsequent meeting, instruction became part of facilitation.

DEVELOPING THE DIALOGUE: REFLECTION AND INTEGRATION

The *Reconciling Practices* program was initiated in the context of public conversation on international Anglican controversy, in closed door conversation with the Secretary General of the Anglican Communion, and in the boundaried space of facilitated dialogue.

As the agenda of each meeting unfolded, a familiar rhythm emerged as Jacques remained constant in his role as facilitator. He ensured each person had space to express themselves and be heard. When he felt an individual was not heard he would check with them on whether his perception was correct and gave them space to clarify their statement. Jacques would often reflect back to the speaker what he understood and ask them to check his listening and understanding. At key moments of the dialogue Jacques would summarize what he noticed had unfolded in the dialogue especially when the group "got stuck" or an impasse was reached. As a facilitator he took seriously a commitment to create space for the participants to "work out" issues directly with one another. Along with improvising the design of the overall program, Jacques was always open to improvising the agenda of individual sessions. Such improvisation often emerged when the energy of the group was waning or when there were indications that the conversation was moving in an unexpected direction. Facilitators should not shy away from naming this and should always be open to taking an unscheduled break, creating space for reflection, rest, and discernment with the other facilitators toward the next step.

At the end of each two-day gathering time was always set aside, generally an hour or two, for reflection on the participants initial expectations for the meeting and their actual experience of the dialogue. This had a twofold function. First, it provided opportunity for individual reflection. Each participant, and the facilitators, were afforded opportunity to do an initial reflection on what happened for them during the dialogue and to articulate, as best they could, their state as they were preparing to leave the meeting. This is not simply an opportunity for reflection but also, in the best of circumstances, it provides participants with resources for integrative work. Participants are often very busy, and often it is easy for them to become immersed back into daily life without much reflection. Naming how the process went and naming one's state of mind as one leaves empowers participants, not only to re-enter the rhythm of life, but to take with them an awareness of why they are feeling a particular way. It can also help participants integrate the skills they are learning into ongoing life and ministry.

Second, reflection at the end of each two-day meeting provided opportunity for group reflection. Individual reflection shared in the group, under facilitation, can create an aggregated picture of the state and development of the group. To what extent is there a sense of community, even amidst deep division, being formed in this process? Given the experience of this meeting, what direction or what topic might the next gathering begin with or work toward? In our experience of *Reconciling Practices*, this end-of-gathering reflection often created a deep realization of the intractable nature of the divisions within the body of Christ and, somewhat paradoxically, a commitment to reconvene again. Indeed, it was in such reflective mode that the desire to have more meetings and visit other seminaries emerged.

At the end of a facilitated meeting and, in this case, at the end of a three-year facilitated dialogue, it is important to get some emotional distance from the experience and de-brief the whole. The hope in debrief is that the experience of dialogue can be integrated into ongoing formation and witness. The hope, in other words, is that such deep work can be integrated into one's understanding of one's self, one's understanding of one's self in community, and one's practice in Christian ministry. The alternative to reflection and integration is to "set aside" or "shelve" the experience in the hope that at some future stage it might become a resource for growth. Too often the opportunity for integration is not taken. The experience remains shelved in its unprocessed, raw state.

De-briefing may be timed for the last session of the last meeting after a good hour or an overnight break to get some distance from the experience. Or it may be timed for a separate special gathering after the completion of the dialogue. An advantage of the latter is that there has been a lot of space for individual reflection. The intensity of the encounter is allowed to diminish allowing for clearer seeing and thinking. A disadvantage of allowing time to pass is that the energy and vision of the dialogue may be somewhat lost. Our last pre-Lambeth Conference meeting took place at Nashotah House at the end of February 2020. Our agenda was focused on presenting our experience in a seminar for bishops at the conference in Canterbury, England. The plan was that we would do a final de-briefing session after the seminar or at a special final session in the fall. However, the coronavirus pandemic intervened. The Lambeth Conference was twice postponed and, thus, so was our presentation and final debriefing session. At the time of writing, neither the conference nor our final debrief have taken place.

For some on *Reconciling Practices*, the process changed their very understanding of ministry and vocation. For others they found ways of finding fellowship in the absence of agreement. For some participants, presentation at a Lambeth Conference was not something, in the end, they could take part in in good conscience. For one participant, these complexities meant that he did not take part in our final meeting together. As with many dialogues in the context of deep division, the future is unclear. What is clear is that this work remains difficult. Yet, if we are to claim a catholicity of faith, practice love of neighbor, and open our lives to the work of the Holy Spirit, such work remains important. Across traditions, internationally and nationally, and across differences in our communities, the world awaits a practice of reconciliation that holds one another in love amidst the deepest of disagreements. While not perfect, *Reconciling Practices* gave a glimpse of that possibility. In the following chapters you will further discover glimpses of what those practices might be in walking together (chapter 3), in listening together in scripture and prayer (chapter 4), and in witnessing to reconciliation (chapter 5).

3.

WALKING TOGETHER

TESTIMONY AMIDST DEEP DISAGREEMENT

The *Reconciling Practices* cohort met five times over three years. For different reasons only two of the cohort were present on every occasion. Despite this, until the very end, a sense of group identity emerged as participants learned to witness to one another and even pray with and for each other. Hundreds of hours were spent together, in prayer, in conversation, in writing, in storytelling, and in grace. We have walked together in step, and we have walked together out of step. We have walked closely together, and we have walked at a distance from one another. Always we have acknowledged the divisions and the stories, the anxieties and the possibilities for trust, and the need for God's presence and power.

DIVISIONS AND STORIES

What are we doing?

We all said yes to something, even if we had no idea where it might lead: five seminaries, ten seminarians, all chosen to join a cohort walking together across difference, across division, across pain still deeply felt. Some of us from The Episcopal Church, some from the Anglican Church in North America, still others from the Continuum, all of us holding, however tightly or not, to the identity *Anglican*. But what are we doing?

It didn't take long for us to ask that question the first time. Walking together? Yes, but haltingly. Praying together? Yes, but not without disagreement. Reconciling? Yes, but not in the way any of us expected. What are we doing? We are witnessing to one another. We are witnessing our stories, and each other's. We are witnessing our pain and our hope. And now we, the *Reconciling Practices* participants, are witnessing to you.

My bishop says this thing at communion: 'The Table of the Lord is set, and when it is prepared they will come from the north, from the south, from the east and from the west, but they will come and will eat together.' The center is Christ. We are all so different, coming to the center, but Christ unites us—that compass is expansive, there's room for all kinds of people, and the way we come together and talk, we're coming toward the center. As we arrived for our first meeting and started introductions, we may have seen ourselves and one another less as individuals with particular stories and more as "representatives" of various "constituencies:" five seminaries, "conservatives" vs. "liberals," "Catholics" vs. "evangelicals," men and women, those with a "traditional" vs. "progressive" viewpoint on human sexuality, etc. I almost feel as if our particularities are what make us universal. My story, your story, the specifics of who we are and how we each arrived at this table, are vital to understand what we have been doing.

—Jill

At our first meeting, we were all brought face to face with the realities of our divisions, just as we were all beginning to get to know one another. We brought anxieties, hopes, and questions. Were all of us valid at this table? Would my voice, even as a Christian who is gay, count just as much as anyone else's? Could I trust this group with my pain? I imagine similar thoughts were going through everyone else's heads as well.

—Will

Our first meeting was in the context of the Center for Anglican Communion Studies, Mollegen Forum at VTS. In powerful words, Panelist and Secretary-General of the Anglican Communion, the Most Rev. Dr. Josiah Idowu-Fearon, helped our group to better understand the realities of division within the Anglican Communion, even before our group had the chance to get to know one another past our categorical identities of denomination and seminary. After a few hours together, the path became clear. How could we ever orient ourselves toward each other without knowing one another's stories?

I had to hear the whole story of Bill's church and how it got separated, just as he had to understand my own story as an LGBT Christian.

—Jill

We were invited to testify to our faith journeys. We were all still rather guarded with our personal stories—not being too vulnerable about ourselves even if we were willing to show our cards in terms of where we aligned on the contentious issues. Yet, it is impossible to reconcile practices if the practices themselves go unnamed. Part of the work of the first session was to learn how to occupy the same room, as a group of Anglicans with different liturgical practices and opinions, even if it was just our categorical identities of denomination and sending seminary/university. But we had begun the work. We had begun to witness.

ANXIETY AND TRUST

A few "new" people came in for the second session: Mason, Travis, and Jacques. This led to another round of questions. What are we doing? We came to it again in our second meeting. What are reconciling practices? What even *is* reconciliation? Could we reconcile around something even if it's not an agreement among ourselves?

Here is what was at stake in the first session: were each of us going to be "valid" at this table? At the second session, what was at stake became a bigger question. Where were each of us coming from? What did we believe, where were our loyalties, and how far was too far to push one another? In the first session, we had begun to witness to one another. As we continued, we deepened our awareness that each testimony sat within "systems" that had made us. We also became more aware and more able to name the sources of anxiety within ourselves and within the "system" of our group.

At our second meeting, we investigated our differences. This was, and is, so much easier said than done. We talked of scripture and our relationship to it, spoke of what makes a human, what honoring dignity and the image of God in one another required of us, and whether the Church needed to be of one mind. But none of these were spoken of conceptually or without emotion. They were part of our stories. They were beliefs that had caused us pain or led to our liberation. Theology had effects on our lives. And so, the conversation was heated, filled with emotion and truth. We were not talking about ideas. We were talking about each other.

As we continued to share through the difficulty, there was a sense that the room was willing to take on the true weight of things. Through testimony and prayer, we had arrived at a place of trust. It is one thing to say one's piece, but it is another thing for those words to land on soft hearts. If someone is going to share something that some will find controversial, will others be willing to stand that and survive as a group? The answer we slowly reached in this session was, simply, yes.

> Toward the end of the session on the first day, I expressed that, given people's views so different from my own, and the way that I feel that my identity and human dignity is at stake or being rejected by their views, I would not be comfortable taking communion from them if they were a priest. I couldn't accept priestly ministrations from them nor accept them into fellowship. When I said this, I felt almost a sense that there was no way out. The only thing I could think to do was that I knew I had to reach out to someone who was completely on the other side of things, as I saw it. That person was Bill. We had to make a personal connection if the dialogue was going to continue. Ever since then this experience has been deeply formative. I keep coming back to the choice to make a personal, intimate connection with that which I perceive to be the farthest away from me.

> —Jill

I think some of us including myself had been entertaining some (in retrospect) naive notions about eucharistic fellowship as a potential source of unity or a place where unity or a call to unity in the Spirit might be revealed. Jill's comments were a fitting challenge to these ideas.

—Peter

In sidebar conversations we came to realize that a fundamental source of our disagreement, theologically speaking, was that there were different and irreconcilable human anthropologies and understandings of human dignity. We all came to realize that there was no easy resolution to these issues and that efforts to convince one another to change or even moderate our opinions was, humanly speaking, impossible. We began to recognize that this might not be why God had called us together.

It was heartbreaking for me, to realize that we weren't going to agree. I was heartbroken. But there was a point toward the end when Jacques Hadler asked, do we want to continue meeting? There was a verbal assent from everyone. We all wanted to keep showing up. There was a desire to continue meeting. The day this fails is the day we stop showing up for one another. My initial assumptions about this process were deconstructed, but I think because of that we were able to build on a better foundation: we want to continue to meet. Requantifying failure and success as not meaning that everyone ends up sharing the same beliefs.

—**Emily**

I wrote this down from the first day of the second meeting. 'Reconciliation may never mean we change our minds.' I can't name a particular turning point, but it's reshaped and redefined reconciliation for me. Before I thought of it as a static point where everything gets returned to "normal." Now for me it means, being reconciled to things as they are and continuing to show up for that. Reconciliation is not restoration, but it's that we'll keep showing up and participate in a life of faith together given the limitations of the situation we're in.

—**Cate**

As we regathered, we then had to ask the question, if eucharistic fellowship was not even possible as a way of reaching across differences, how could we build a bridge? We individually began to reflect on the reality of ourselves as causing hurt to one another, even if we hadn't intended to. It was when we began to name this hurt that we became a group. We had committed to keep witnessing to and with one another.

HONESTY AND LITURGY

> At the first session, I expressed the desire to meet more frequently than once a year if we were to really lean into reconciliation as a group, and by the second year the group had come to the collective decision that meeting more often was desirable both for deepening our fellowship and working further toward reconciliation.
>
> **—Aaron**

At our third meeting, we started by discussing how we could continue our witness to one another even while our honesty caused each other pain. One of our goals at this meeting was to develop liturgical resources for reconciling across difference. In our liturgical planning session, we passed ideas back and forth. The process was very fraught. Only three of us had taken a liturgy course at that point. The "experts" offered their input, but they also made space and encouraged every-one. We sought consensus on liturgical decisions rather than voting.

We decided unanimously on designing a eucharistic liturgy. This decision was taken in the knowledge that it was unlikely that we, as a group, would share in eucharistic fellowship. Such honesty, however, bore fruit and enabled more careful thinking about the meaning of words, rites, and rituals. We continued to ask hard questions about what was possible and kept in mind the difficulties that each other might experi-ence. We were only able to do this because, from the beginning, we had witnessed to one another. We knew one another's stories.

> The liturgical work was a turning point for me. My own church uses an older prayer book and is not participating in conversa-tions about liturgical revision. But we were working on something that was authentic to our group. This . . . took the pressure off: to realize that this is a work in each of our own internal lives and in reconciliation within our group. We were . . . not . . . going out and solving the disagreements between our churches. It also gave me a sense of a

common goal we could work toward and celebrate together.

—**Mason**

The liturgy planning was a prayerful process. It even involved praying about how to pray! Again, the experience of shared work brought us together, listening to one another's stories about worship, expectations for prayer, and what each of us brought to an experience of liturgy.

> I have felt that group prayer has been the infrastructure that has kept us together. Amid the pain that is still present in our disagreement, prayer is the touchstone that reminds us we are each adopted into God's family by grace. We are each adopted into our Anglican identities. In group prayer, we are all becoming gradually attuned to God's will and purposes for us, which is a belonging together in the body of Christ amid our pain.
>
> —**Alice**

The liturgy produced by the group is reproduced in this workbook for your review. As it turned out, we could witness to one another and we could pray with one another. We could not, however, break bread in Holy Communion with one another.

> . . . everyone was "fried." But also, we are growing in charity and awareness of how we hurt people. It is hard to see one's self as a sinner. This is a way to learn how to love one another better. Our institutions may continue to diverge as they have done. We can still love each other. Reconciliation is not restoration.
>
> **—Peter**

WALKING TOGETHER AND THE LAMBETH CONFERENCE

By our fourth meeting we knew that our seminar proposal to the Lambeth Conference 2020 was accepted. We would be presenting a report on our journey together to bishops of the Anglican Communion. We would invite them into conversation and offer them the resources we had produced. This was a complicated prospect. Some of the bishops of our churches were not invited and some were. This put some of us in a difficult position. In the end, some would choose not to attend the Lambeth Conference because their bishops were not invited. Yet, a care for one another had developed over the years and something happened that we could not have predicted. Those on opposite sides of debates, particularly around human sexuality, were concerned to represent each other's positions clearly, honestly, and with integrity. Those who would not attend the conference had confidence that those who would attend could present an honest picture of the work and discernment we had done together. If this was to be done, we would have to prepare not only for our presentation but for the culture that we would encounter when the Communion meets formally.

As we explored together the themes chosen for the conference and the forms the conference would take, we also explored the likely anxieties and controversies that would be dominant at the Lambeth Conference. We had emotional and cultural preparation to do. We would be entering into deep contestation and contested space. As we did this work together, at our fourth meeting, we came to realize that the place we had reached as a group with irreconcilable differences was not the place that our churches or Communion(s) had reached. In an effort to crystallize the work we had done and the distance there likely would be between the culture of the conference and our group, we started to put on paper our own understandings of reconciliation as we came to the end of our process (see chapter 5). What was it that we now understood to be reconciliation? How would these definitions differ from what our churches and Communion taught? What would our experience and understanding bring to bishops who had their own assumptions about what reconciliation is or could be?

We had begun our journey together at VTS in conversation with the Secretary General of the Anglican Communion, and it seemed somehow fitting that we would close our final meeting at VTS with a representative from the Anglican Church of North America (ACNA). We had conversation with this leader over dinner. Our formation in *Reconciling Practices* had taught us to read our own anxieties and the anxieties of others. This did not mean that we could not be surprised by anxiety. Even at this late stage of our process together we could be surprised by anxiety. Not everyone felt welcomed to the dinner conversation. The dinner setup was more formal than some of us were expecting. In this moment, differences in class as well as theology and ecclesiology were raised. One of our number left quietly. She was uncomfortable with the setting for this conversation. This pointed both to the trust we had built in our processes of meeting but also pointed to the insecurities and anxieties still at work in our divisions. In these processes of dialogue, attention and communication is key at every single step and in every single space.

The conversation itself was preparatory for the Lambeth Conference in ways that even the facilitators of *Reconciling Practices* might not have anticipated. The tone here was different to the tone in our closed-door gatherings. In many respects both guests, at the beginning and end of our time together, had a similar style and confidence. In this occasion, some of us read a good deal of anxiety in our guest and some of us experienced a renewed level of anxiety in this conversation. Our ways of listening and walking and witnessing were practiced. Our guest came with a different style and different tone. This did nothing to lower levels of anxieties. It only served to raise the anxiety levels for some in the group. Some in the group were at liberty to speak and engage with the guest; others felt inhibited or even afraid.

Asked by Robert Heaney to share something of his journey and the journey of his church, our guest did so with confidence and clarity. In effect, his ministry and the ministry of his congregation had "moved beyond" the "presenting issues" of human sexuality and the divisions at work in the broad Anglican family in the U.S.A. Other issues were now the focus of his witness and that of his congregation. Everyone in the group could agree that ecumenical cooperation, race relations, and inter-religious understanding were vital areas of work for the sake of justice and witness amidst people of faith. Some in the group found such a vision inspiring. Others found the vision disturbing as it was based on a decisive decision "to move on" from the very controversies that the *Reconciling Practices* cohort were continuing to grapple with. This conversation and the style of this conversation was a moment where we all could, in small part, anticipate the nature of a Lambeth Conference and the likely nature of our responses. It was clear that further, deeper, and more deliberate work in preparing for Lambeth was needed. How could we develop both resilience and a diplomatic presence in Canterbury?

We met for a fifth and final time at Nashotah House for a session that would focus particularly on preparation for the Lambeth Conference. What would be the design of our seminar? What would we say? How would we say it? Who would speak? How would those not present feel that the seminar would represent their part in the *Reconciling Practices* journey? In many ways this was a meeting focused on a specific task and outcome. Four foci shaped this meeting. We needed to work on polishing our *Reconciling Practices* publication that we would present as part of the Lambeth Conference seminar. Further work needed to be done in preparing ourselves and preparing to monitor and regulate our anxiety in the context of a Lambeth conference. The design particulars of the seminar would have to be put down on paper. Then, in this final meeting before Lambeth, we would seek to create space for reflection on the journey up until this point.

While this was a more task driven meeting as we prepared our seminar together, deeper moments of solidarity seemed to emerge alongside deeper moments of anxiety. We were a group. We would be representing each other. There was recognition that for some the conference would be a frightening experience. There was resolve to support one another and to care for one another. By the end of this our third year of meeting together, we were able to say, "I love you . . . and I've hurt you." We had come to realize that this is what real relationship in Christ looked like. This was a new way of learning to love one another, even across division. The power of holding love and hurt together had become our witness.

During this meeting we had dinner with a key bishop from The Episcopal Church (TEC) who is part of the so-called "Communion Partners" group. This is a group of bishops from TEC and the Anglican Church of Canada that support a traditional or conservative understanding of human sexuality and seek the broadest practice of fellowship within Anglicanism. Again, here was an opportunity to prepare ourselves for the Lambeth Conference. The tone of this visiting bishop was different. His woundedness came from a desire to be loyal to TEC and to accept the dominant position on human sexuality at work in official Anglican Communion statements and discernment. He occupied a distinct space. He was a minority in his own church yet aligned with official positions in the broader Communion. His story and testimony, though distinct, was familiar to us all, and his humility in telling his story and explaining his position was something we all had been learning to do over the past three years. Here might be an example of what Robert Heaney called being present in "diplomatic mode." Our seminaries had taught us so much. Yet, it had not taught us how to do this work and for some of us this work had become the most important endeavor we had undertaken in our time as seminarians.

AN EPILOGUE WITHOUT RESOLUTION

We were, and are, unlikely companions, deep friends, partners in Christ. Whether over drinks and pizza or in the individual "check-ins" we did at the beginning of every meeting or in the midst of the most harrowing discussion of theological pain, our friendships persist. They ground us in Christ. We've discovered that joyful fellowship is as important as our "real" work and that rest is vital to coming back to the table. Though some have missed sessions, they have always been welcomed back into the group. That is the power of these friendships, of relationship in Christ, built through our shared stories. It is enough to keep us together.

So what are we doing? Though it is tempting to pretend otherwise, there is no rosy epilogue. But there is hope. At the end of these three years, none of us have changed our minds on the issues which brought us together. Some decided they could not attend the Lambeth Conference. One decided that he could not come to our final meeting. There has been no resolution of division or difference. There have been no conversions from one "side" to the other. But there has been a transformation. The transformation has been in how we seek Christ in one another. We seek Christ in relationship, in commitment, in communion. When we speak of those things that sow division among us, we are no longer talking about ideas only, or positions on issues. We recognize that we are talking about one another, holding the weight of each story as we try to listen for the truth.

What we have learned is the power of telling our stories, and finding a glimmer of the Gospel in each of them. What we have learned is that trusting each other with our pain opens the door to the Holy Spirit. We have learned that reconciliation is a constant process, not an arrival at agreement. We have learned to seek God in one another, and perhaps that is enough.

LISTENING TOGETHER
READING SCRIPTURE AMIDST DEEP DISAGREEMENT

As has already been seen, our group came together over three years to seek an understanding of reconciliation and discern what that means in practice. This group would never have come together without the *Reconciling Practices* program. We witnessed to one another, but we also reflected on scripture together and prayed together. In seeking God in one another, we sought to read scripture together and pray together. In this chapter, we invite you to reflect on scripture and to pray. You, like us, may be able to do this in a context of division or by convening a group made up of people who represent a particular division present in your community.

Given the deep divisions in the *Reconciling Practices* cohort we were unable to use all of the liturgical material in this chapter. We could read scripture and pray together, but we could not share in the Eucharist together. We could imagine sharing together at the Lord's table, but we could not do it in practice. The disagreements at work in our midst had, then, not only implications for how we read scripture or understood the nature of the Church but had implications for how we understood what made the validity of the Eucharist.

GLORY AND HUMILITY: A BIBLE STUDY ON JOHN 12:27–36a

As he speaks to the crowd gathered, Jesus has entered triumphantly into Jerusalem for the celebration of the Passover. The crowd gathered is diverse: "among those who went up to worship at the festival were some Greeks" (12:20), and Jesus himself arrived in the city from Galilee.

> Jesus said, "Now my soul is troubled. And what should I say—'Father, save me from this hour'? No, it is for this reason that I have come to this hour. Father, glorify your name." Then a voice came from heaven, "I have glorified it, and I will glorify it again." The crowd standing there heard

it and said that it was thunder. Others said, "An angel has spoken to him." Jesus answered, "This voice has come for your sake, not for mine. Now is the judgment of this world; now the ruler of this world will be driven out. And I, when I am lifted up from the earth, will draw all people to myself." He said this to indicate the kind of death he was to die. The crowd answered him, "We have heard from the law that the Messiah remains forever. How can you say that the Son of Man must be lifted up? Who is this Son of Man?" Jesus said to them, "The light is with you for a little longer. Walk while you have the light, so that the darkness may not overtake you. If you walk in the darkness, you do not know where you are going. While you have the light, believe in the light, so that you may become children of light."

In John's Gospel, glory and humility sit together. God is glorified in humility. A common pursuit is walking as children of the light. Both these themes, humility and being children of light, have taught us something about the work of reconciliation.

Jesus' self-sacrifice is unique. The call to emulate Jesus, in a self-sacrificial manner, is both at the heart of the Gospel and the heart of the pain the church has caused. To read these verses and to faithfully interpret them, we must depend on the Spirit of God. Re-read

John 12:27–36a. Ask God to open your heart to the voice of the Spirit as you read and reflect.

Reflect on the questions below:

1. What might it mean, in your life, to practice a commitment to God's will over your own will? How might you center the glorification of God in your life, even and especially when your soul is troubled?

2. St. Irenaeus said, "The glory of God is the human person fully alive, and the life of the human person consists in beholding God." We hear in this passage that the full life of the world arises from the death of Jesus. How do you understand the death of Christ in your life as a Christian?

3. If self-offering is the means to drawing close to Christ, how do you practice self-offering in your life?

4. The "kind of death" Jesus died exalted him. What "kind of death" was Jesus to die?

5. Jesus calls us to become children of light. What does it mean to "believe in the light?" Have you ever experienced being overtaken by darkness? How did it feel? How did you cultivate an ability to see the light in the midst of the dark?

After reflecting on these questions or discussing these questions with others, take some time in silent prayer. After about five minutes of silence say this prayer:

> Lord Jesus Christ, in being lifted up you drew all people to yourself: help us to embody the humility with which you offered yourself, that we may be made true children of light, to the glory of your name. Amen.

LOVE AMIDST CONTROVERSY: A BIBLE STUDY ON MARK 12:28–34

One of the scribes came near and heard them disputing with one another, and seeing that he answered them well, he asked him, "Which commandment is the first of all?" Jesus answered, "The first is, 'Hear, O Israel: the Lord our God, the Lord is one; you shall love the Lord your God with all your heart, and with all your soul, and with all your mind, and with all your strength.' The second is this, 'You shall love your neighbor as yourself.' There is no other commandment greater than these." Then the scribe said to him, "You are right, Teacher; you have truly said that 'he is one, and besides him there is no other;' and 'to love him with all the heart, and with all the understanding, and with all the strength,' and 'to love one's neighbor as oneself,'—this is much more important than all whole burnt offerings and sacrifices." When Jesus saw that he answered wisely, he said to him, "You are not far from the kingdom of God." After that no one dared to ask him any question.

Jesus' instruction takes place in a context of conflict. The Sadducees and Jesus had been arguing about the meaning of resurrection. Jesus' response is the Sh'ma, a distillation of the Law: God is one, love God, love your neighbor.

Often, we engage with one another as "other," but Jesus invites us to engage with the other as self. In this passage, we hear that "besides God, there is no other." When we read this line, we often assume Jesus means that there are no other gods. Yet, perhaps, Jesus means here to remind us that if we love God, we cannot be separated from one another. If we love God, the differences which divide us are obsolete. The relational quality of loving God and neighbor transcends the worldly disputes which create an "Other" out of community. This relational quality of loving God and loving neighbor is at the heart of living as people of God's kingdom. In times of conflict, the heart of reconciliation must be greeting one's neighbor with this relational love, regardless of where one stands along lines of dispute. When we come together amidst disagreement, the manner with which we conduct ourselves in conflict is of more ultimate (eschatological) importance than whether we are "right" or "wrong" within the conflict. As you reflect on this passage, ask God to open your heart to the voice of the Spirit as you read and reflect.

1. How is the "one-ness" of God related to the commandment to love God and to love neighbor?

2. What does this passage identify as a foundation goal of our religion? In an Anglican context, what are additional foundations of faith which all Anglicans share? How might searching for these common foundations affect our experience of conflict in the Anglican Communion?

3. As well as finding things that unite Anglicans, we too can focus on things that divide us. We can exhibit a tendency to "other" those we disagree with or think we disagree with. How do you understand "othering" and how does it play out in your context?

4. Ideally, to love God and neighbor is at the heart of faith for Christians. How might we assume the best intentions of our partners in conversation? What practices will help me greet my neighbor with love while

simultaneously assuming they are doing the same?

5. In what ways can we honor difference without falling into practices of "othering"? Read Colossians 2:1–19. How do you understand diversity within the church and the idea that Christians are knit together in love?

After reflecting on these questions or discussing these questions with others, take some time in silent prayer. After about five minutes of silence, say this prayer:

> Lord Jesus Christ, in whom God and our neighbor are brought together: grant us grace to love God so deeply with our heart, soul, mind, and strength, and our neighbor as ourselves, that in so doing we may discover that in you there is no "Other," to the glory of your name. Amen.

AN ORDER OF WORSHIP FOR THE EVENING

The church is dark when the service is to begin.

Officiant	Bless the Lord who forgives all our sins.
People	**God's mercy endures forever.**

Here is sung the Phos hilaron *or some other suitable evening hymn.*
A short, suitable passage of scripture is read.
The following psalm is read in unison, pausing at the asterisk.

PSALM 119:49–56

Memor esto verbi tui

Zayin

49 Remember your word to your servant, *
    because you have given me hope.

50 This is my comfort in my trouble, *
    that your promise gives me life.

51 The proud have derided me cruelly, *
    but I have not turned from your law.

52 When I remember your judgements of old, *
    O Lord, I take great comfort.

53 I am filled with a burning rage, *
    because of the wicked who forsake your law.

54 Your statues have been like sons to me *
    wherever I have lived as a stranger.

55 I remember your Name in the night, O Lord, *
    and dwell upon your law.

56 This is how is has been with me, *
    because I have kept your commandments.

COLLECT FOR A TIME OF PENITENCE

Officiant: Let us pray.

Almighty and merciful God, kindle within us the fire of love, that by its cleansing flame we may be purged of all our sins and made worthy to worship you in spirit and in truth; through Jesus Christ our Lord. Amen.

LITANY OF RECONCILIATION

Litanist   Holy God, you formed us
            from the dust:

People   **In your image and likeness.**

Litanist   You redeemed us from sin and death:

People   **By the cross of Jesus Christ.**

Litanist   Through the water of baptism:

People   **You clothed us with righteousness
            and counted us among your
            children.**

Litanist   But we have squandered the
            inheritance of your saints:

People   **And we have wandered far
            in a land that is waste.**

The people enter a time of guided contemplation.

Litanist Therefore, O Lord,

People **We turn to you in sorrow and repentance.**

Litanist Receive us again into the arms of your mercy,

People **And restore us to the blessed company of your faithful.**

Litanist Through him in whom you have redeemed the world,

People **Your son, our Savior Jesus Christ. Amen.**

All say the absolution in unison:

**Almighty God,
receive our confession
of sorrow and of faith,
strengthen us in all goodness,
and by the power of the Holy Spirit
keep us in eternal life. Amen.**

Litanist Now there is rejoicing in heaven;

People **For we were lost, and are found; we were dead, and are now alive in Christ Jesus our Lord. The Lord has put away all our sins.**

Officiant   Let us pray.

Almighty, everlasting God, let our prayer in your sight be as incense, the lifting up of our hands as the evening sacrifice. Give us grace to behold you, present in your Word and Sacraments, and to recognize you in the lives of those around us. Stir up in us the flame of that love which burned in the heart of your Son as he bore his passion, and let it burn in us to eternal life and to the ages of ages. Amen.

All together say the blessing:

> **The Lord bless us and keep us. Amen.**
>
> **The Lord make his face to shine upon us and be gracious to us. Amen.**
>
> **The Lord lift up his countenance upon us and give us peace. Amen.**

Officiant   Let us go forth in the name of Christ.
People   **Thanks be to God.**

A EUCHARISTIC LITURGY FOR A TIME OF FRAGMENTATION

Here follow brief rubrics for a eucharistic liturgy for a time of fragmentation. These rubrics are not comprehensive, but rather offer shape for communal worship during a time of division within one's community. At appropriate moments, we offer suggestions for prayer, Scripture, and music which we find echo the themes and emotions of our work and life together. Please note that the pronouns used for God in this liturgy are consistent with those of The Book of Common Prayer 1979 of The Episcopal Church. The worship leader may choose to substitute these pronouns for the name "God."

I. GATHERING IN THE LORD'S NAME

We suggest using the opening acclamation for Lent, as appointed in The Book of Common Prayer 1979. This acclamation emphasizes mutuality in sin and the abundance of God's mercy.

Officiant   Bless the Lord who forgives all our sins.
People   **His mercy endures forever.**

Though the collect of the day is always appropriate, below we offer additional options which highlight the themes of sin, unity, and prayer for those who hurt us.

COLLECT FOR GOOD FRIDAY
(ECUSA, Book of Common Prayer 1979, 221)

Almighty God, we pray you graciously to behold this your family, for whom our Lord Jesus Christ was willing to be betrayed, and given into the hands of sinners, and to suffer death upon the cross; who now lives and reigns with you and the Holy Spirit, one God, for ever and ever. Amen.

COLLECT FOR THE UNITY OF THE CHURCH
(ECUSA, Book of Common Prayer 1979, 818)

O God the Father of our Lord Jesus Christ, our only Savior, the Prince of Peace: Give us grace seriously to lay to heart the great dangers we are in by our unhappy divisions; take away all hatred and prejudice, and whatever else may hinder us from godly union and concord; that, as there is but one Body and one Spirit, one hope of our calling, one Lord, one Faith, one Baptism, one God and Father of us all, so we may be all of one heart and of one soul, united in one holy bond of truth and peace, of faith and charity, and may with one mind and one mouth glorify thee; through Jesus Christ our Lord. Amen.

COLLECT FOR OUR ENEMIES
(ECUSA, Book of Common Prayer 1979, 814)

O God, the Father of all, whose Son commanded us to love our enemies: Lead them and us from prejudice to truth: deliver them and us from hatred, cruelty, and revenge; and in your good time enable us all to stand reconciled before you, through Jesus Christ our Lord. Amen.

II. PROCLAIMING AND RESPONDING TO THE WORD OF GOD

The proclamation and response may include readings, songs, talk, dance, music, other art forms, silence. A reading from the Gospel is always included.

Suggested Scripture Readings appropriate for the ethos of the liturgy include:

1.   HEBREW BIBLE

   Genesis 33

   Micah 6:1–8

2.   EPISTLE

   1 Corinthians 1:10–17

   1 Corinthians 11:23– or 27–33

   2 Corinthians 5:11– or 13–21

   Galatians 3

   Ephesians 4

   Philippians 2

   Colossians 3

   Hebrews 12

3.   GOSPEL

   Mark 10:35–45

   John 17:6a, 15–23

   Luke 22:23– or 24–32

   Luke 6:30–42

III. PRAYER FOR THE WORLD AND THE CHURCH

During a time of prayer, it is appropriate to include a rite to respond directly to the division in your community. This rite may take many forms based on one's cultural context and particular situation. Some possibilities follow.

OPTION 1:
COMMUNITY CONFESSION AND ABSOLUTION

In the rite below, Parts A and B may be taken by respective parties across the lines of division. Once the first group recites Part A and is absolved by the second group, the two groups switch roles and repeat the rite.

Part A: **I confess to Almighty God, Father, Son and Holy Spirit, before the angels and saints in heaven, and to you my brothers and sisters, that I have sinned exceedingly in thought, word and deed, by my fault, by my own fault, by my own most grievous fault. God have mercy upon me and forgive me. Brothers and sisters, pray for me to the Lord our God.**

Part B: **May the Almighty God have mercy upon you and forgive you of all your sin.**

If a priest is present, they may use the absolution below after the confession above.

Priest: Almighty God have mercy upon you, forgive you all your sins, and bring you to everlasting life. The almighty and merciful Lord grant us pardon, absolution, and remission of all our sins. Amen.

OPTION 2:
INTERPERSONAL CONFESSION
BETWEEN INDIVIDUALS

Members of the congregation greet one another by saying, "I love you, and I [have] hurt you" *and responding,* "I forgive you."

They then exchange a sign of the peace.

OPTION 3:
CONFESSION BETWEEN DIVIDED PARTIES

This may take the same form as the above (Option 2). A brief naming of the source of division and pain between each party may be included, followed by a communal recitation of the absolution and sharing of the peace.

FOOT-WASHING

The rite should begin with corporate confession and absolution.

The Maundy Thursday rite may be used. If doing so, the rite may be introduced within the particulars of your community's division, emphasizing that mutual foot-washing calls all members of the community to humble themselves and to trust the other in return.

IV. Exchange the Peace

Either here or elsewhere in the service, all greet one another in the name of the Lord.

V. Prepare the Table

Some of those present prepare the table; the bread, the cup of wine, and other offerings are placed upon the table.

VI. Make Eucharist

The Celebrant gives thanks to God for the work of creation and revelation through Jesus Christ; recalls before God, when appropriate, the particular occasion being celebrated; incorporates or adapts the Proper Preface of the Day, if desired. It is appropriate to adapt the Proper Preface to reflect themes of reconciliation and restoration. If doing so, you might reference Jesus as the "first-born of all creation, for in him all things were created, in heaven and on earth . . . He is before all things, and in him all things hold together" (Col. 1); make reference to Esau and Jacob as God's work in restoring relationship (Gen. 33); or make reference to the one who sits upon the throne making "all things new" (Rev. 21).

VII. Break the Bread and Share the Gifts of God

The Body and Blood of Our Lord are shared in a reverent manner. After all have received, any of the Sacrament that remains is then consumed. The distribution of the elements may be choreographed to embody restoration and reintegration within the community present. This may be done by inviting members across lines of strife to participate in distributing the bread and wine to one another. Individual members of the community who have caused division may distribute the sacrament to the rest of the congregation as a sign of reincorporation into the Body of Christ.

VIII. Benediction

The celebrant may desire to send the congregation forth with a prayer reflecting the particular work done during the service. If so, the sending prayer and blessing might include reference to the division among the congregation and its ritual healing, as well as work still necessary to continue reconciliation. The sending prayer should include a reminder of our hope in Christ's reconciling love.

5.

WITNESSING TOGETHER

DEFINING RECONCILIATION AMIDST DEEP DISAGREEMENT

When our conversations began, we were unsure of what to expect. Perhaps some of us had vague notions of how the conversations might proceed, as well as vague hopes for what might come about through our efforts. Looking back, most of us shared the assumption that over the course of our meetings and conversations, we would be able to reach some level of concrete resolution, even if that resolution was to decide that our conversations were no longer worth having. Speaking honestly, members of our group from both sides of the theological divide believed we could change the views of the other if only we could tell our stories and share our viewpoints powerfully enough. This has not been the case.

The realization that we could not reach agreement was initially heartbreaking and discouraging. Upon further reflection, conversation, and prayer, new possibilities for what reconciliation could look like began to emerge. As we walked together, witnessed together, and worshiped together, we began to learn more about each other's beliefs. More importantly, we began to learn more about each other.

Hours of difficult, vulnerable conversation left us with two deeply held truths. We loved each other and yet reconciliation would not mean conversion of beliefs. Our central crisis was such: what is the hope of reconciliation in a circumstance in which no agreement can be reached? Yet, our developing relationships, built on care for one another and our mutual love of God and God's church, kept bringing us together in search of what reconciliation could ultimately be.

Below is an attempt by members of our group to describe his or her understanding of what reconciliation is. These definitions have been formed and transformed by the relationships we have built amidst the hurts we have caused, felt, and shared. We have intentionally left the definitions anonymous in order to offer these definitions with as little bias and as much unity as possible.

DEFINITIONS OF RECONCILIATION

Before you read and reflect on these definitions of reconciliation re-read and pray this prayer (from chapter 4):

Lord Jesus Christ, in whom God and our neighbor are brought together: grant us grace to love God so deeply with our heart, soul, mind, and strength, and our neighbor as ourselves, that in so doing we may discover that in you there is no "Other," to the glory of your name. Amen.

Our incorporation into the body of Christ the Reconciler compels us to reach out to others from whom we have been estranged. This is a work of the Cross. It means being willing to experience hurt, to confront the pain that sin and division cause to the body of Christ, to learn how I hurt others, and to encounter Jesus in this. Reconciliation can set aside the anxiety that arises around differences. It is a mutual willingness to know and be known by those with whom I am in conflict. If we ask God, the Holy Spirit will give us grace to take these risks. Listening means becoming open, first, to really understanding the person in front of you, not as a member of a category, but as a unique and precious self.

•

Reconciliation is the literal "bringing together again" of people who have been fractured and divided. God has reconciled us to Himself through Christ, and by His Spirit we are called and brought together in reconciliation to one another. As sinful humanity, we begin to do so by our humble acknowledgement of our "manifold sins and offences" against God and neighbor. We may have to enter into a place of vulnerability and pain in the process, but we do so while inviting the great Comforter, the Holy Spirit, to be and work in our midst to heal division, restore relationships, and raise us to new life in Christ. In short, reconciliation is a God-driven work.

•

When I think of reconciliation, the image that comes to mind is people in the same room together though the door is wide open. It is not forced; it is a choice to stay engaged with the other person. Reconciliation is any work to repair the distance between us and that work is difficult and Holy. It depends on an open heart even when staying in the conversation sometimes breaks your heart. Reconciliation calls us to commit ourselves to the ongoing process of healing.

•

Reconciliation is a process of building personal relationships in the midst of active conflict. This process begins with a self-determination to allow yourself to love and be loved by someone you are in conflict with, even, and especially when, the love is imperfect, incomplete, or painful. The relationship does not seek agreement, but in humility always allows for its possibility with the recognition that I may be wrong. Likewise, reconciliation does not look to eliminate the divide engendered by the conflict but to build relational bridges that transcend the conflict. These bridges in no way displace, replace, or silence the conflict, but coexist with it while opening relational pathways founded on love and our own mutual life in Christ.

•

The intention of reconciliation is not necessarily restoration but rather is the work of learning to be reconciled to things exactly as they are in a state of conflict. If my hope in reconciliation is not to change the hearts of those who disagree with me or to win them over to my side, but rather to simply commit to continuing to gather around the table, I find myself liberated. I become free to show up exactly as myself, and to learn about the whole person standing across from us rather than just seeing them as "Other" defined by a position or opinion.

•

God asks difficult questions through the Holy Scriptures: which of our neighbors do we avoid? What dimensions of God's work do our choices resist? Reconciliation is an uncomfortable enterprise. But avoid discomfort long enough, and the cost will be paid in human suffering. Reconciliation resists any mentality of individuality but instead asks us to, in the words of Pauli Murray, "suffer with and for one another before we will be healed of the sickness of our common history."

•

One of the things our group studied was Family Systems Theory, which is a way of explaining group dynamics. We learned that healthy systems contain individuals of a mature level of self-differentiation amidst anxiety, yet without cutting off. In the context of our group, reconciliation has meant presence to each other and commitment to our conversation amidst our differences, anxiety, and disunity, out of respect for each other and for the importance of the conversation we are having. I have come now to an understanding of reconciliation as commitment: commitment to remaining in community amidst anxiety and commitment to remaining present in conversation amidst disagreement.

•

From the beginning of this experience, our group has had to grapple with the concept of reconciliation in a situation in which beliefs cannot be compromised or combined. I have found deep hope in a continued desire to be together, to share genuinely, and to listen deeply to and with people who hold very different beliefs from my own. Our conversations have frequently been challenging and often devastating. Our group's ability to hold each other in prayer and love has provided hope that, through the grace of God, we can walk together as we continue discerning what reconciliation can and should be.

•

"I love you. And I have hurt you." Reconciliation is not recovery from pain. Nor is it pretending division never happened. It is the absurd belief in God's Grace to overcome that division, that pain. Reconciliation is submission to the demands of our baptism into Jesus' death on a cross. Yet if we too shall taste life after facing death, we shall do it as one, in Christ, together. Christ's resurrected body retains the marks of suffering. So will ours. Reconciliation is the absurd, exhausting belief that those marks of who we have been need not determine who we shall be.

•

As you read these definitions, is there one that you are drawn to above another? Why is that?

REFLECTING ON THE CALL TO RECONCILIATION

As our definitions suggest, we believe that reconciliation is hard, vulnerable, and often frustrating work. We also believe that reconciliation is holy work, deeply centered on the relationships we have built with each other as members of the body of Christ. Together we have listened for how God is inviting us to consider the pain we have caused and received. We have only been able to engage in this work because we have all continually chosen to be present, to risk confronting tension and heartache that we could otherwise have avoided or ignored outright. In our efforts at reconciling, we have each been able to witness to what we believe is true, even when our beliefs are contradictory. Our process and conversations are possible because of our love for each other. We continue to witness to this love each time we are together, trusting the Spirit will continue to bring healing in unexpected ways.

As you read these definitions, spend some time in silence. Reflect with us. Ask the Spirit to draw you into the work of God in the world. Before answering the questions below pray this prayer (from chapter 4):

> Lord Jesus Christ, in whom God and our neighbor are brought together: grant us grace to love God so deeply with our heart, soul, mind, and strength, and our neighbor as ourselves, that in so doing we may discover that in you there is no "Other," to the glory of your name. Amen.

1. What general themes do you see present in our definitions?
2. What differences or potential conflicts do you see?
3. What is your own working definition of reconciliation?
4. How does your experience with reconciliation relate to ours?
5. How might you promote the development of personal relationships with those you are in conflict with?

For further resources and ideas for reconciliatory work in your own context, consult the "further resources" section at the end of this book.

CONCLUSION

Robert S. Heaney

In reading this short account of *Reconciling Practices*, one cannot help be impressed by the spirit and seriousness that these seminarians exhibited in this process. In deep division, a natural and well-tested response is to "cut off" those one disagrees with. This takes place in our personal lives. This takes place in the life of our institutions. This has taken place in Anglican history and in the Anglican Communion.

For the seminaries and seminarians involved in *Reconciling Practices*, we have utmost respect, admiration, and love. They all came from places defined by a cutting off, and they were often being formed in contexts with little or no contact with the divisions at work in the Communion. To lean into division and disagreement is not easy. It is frightening. It is exhausting. It can even be dangerous. These seminarians were prepared to face the depths of division at work in our

Anglican traditions as embodied in the lives and stories of fellow seminarians.

The members of the *Reconciling Practices* cohort are now leaders in the church of Christ. Some have integrated this experience deeply into their understanding and practice of leadership or priesthood. We have learned much from the participants in this process. At the time of the Center for Anglican Communion Studies' 20th anniversary celebration, we summed up our vision as, "promoting and practicing better community for the Communion." That vision was grounded, we were fond of saying, in three imperatives: reflect, resource, reconcile. Today, in the latest iteration of the vision, we say that the Center "resources practices of reconciliation" through equipping international community, empowering intercultural leaders, and enriching Episcopal-Anglican identity. Reconciliation has, in other words, come to the fore of how the Center understands its work and witness in the Church and Communion. In no small part, it is the work and witness of the *Reconciling Practices* cohort that has encouraged this shift.

Even in Christian organizations there is a nervousness on using the language of reconciliation. I share that nervousness. There are enough examples of the word being ill-defined, misused, or cheapened that would justify hesitancy. Yet, the depth of the work done by the *Reconciling Practices* cohort should remind us that it is a holy word. It is a word predicated upon the deep sin and brokenness of our world (Rom. 5:10–21). It is the witness of God in Christ to the world (2

Cor. 5:11–15; Eph. 2:14-22; Col. 1:15–20). It is God's commission to the church throughout the ages (2 Cor. 5:16–17). It is the very work of God to be revealed at the end of the ages (2 Cor. 5:18–21; see Rev. 21:1–6).

> For the love of Christ urges us on, because we are convinced that one has died for all; therefore all have died. And he died for all, so that those who live might live no longer for themselves, but for him who died and was raised for them. From now on, therefore, we regard no one from a human point of view; even though we once knew Christ from a human point of view, we know him no longer in that way. So if anyone is in Christ, there is a new creation: everything old has passed away; see, everything has become new! All this is from God, who reconciled us to himself through Christ, and has given us the ministry of reconciliation. (2 Cor. 5:14–18)

The deep implications of the reconciliatory mission of God are but glimpsed in our communities and our relationships. But, glimpsed they are. In imperfect and in contingent ways we do, in some movements and brief moments, catch a glimpse of God's future. Over a three-year period in the walking, listening, and witnessing of this cohort, we were given a glimpse of a different reality.

The dominant culture in the U.S.A likes to measure things. If it cannot be counted and reduced to data, it is unlikely to be of any significance in the nation or in the neighborhood. It would be comforting to think that the church was a moderating influence on such instrumentalism. It would be inspiring to think that the church could counter such reductionism when necessary. It would be wonderful to think that the church was known as a great humanizing movement within broader cultures that holds up the value of personal encounter, the seemingly inconsequential story, and the small transformations in lives and communities. But, alas, the church and its institutions often collude in reducing life and worth to things that can be measured or weighed.

The *Reconciling Practices* program can be measured. It can be represented in data—number of seminarians in the process; number of seminaries in partnership; hours spent in conversation; dollars spent in staff assistance, hospitality, resources, and travel; product outcomes in publication and dissemination; number of parishioners likely to be impacted by the cohort. That, however, is not a snapshot. It is not a summary. It is reductionism. It is reductionist, first of all, because while it measures some things, the metrics do not measure *other* things. For example, what learning outcomes were at work in *Reconciling Practices*? To what extent did these outcomes shape the participants' understanding of vocation and pastoral practice? But even this understanding of metrics and measurements is reductionist. Indeed, it is a reductionism that tends to dehumanization. For if the work of *Reconciling Practices* has spiritual and relational impact, how might this be measured without falling into a reductionist instrumentalism? For even if it were somehow possible to measure relational depth, personal epiphany, experience of divine grace, confidence in testimony, renewed hermeneutical commitment, refreshed liturgical vision, growing capacity to discern amidst irresolvability, and shifting understandings of Christian vocation—the measurement would be a reduction. For the rich experiences and stories cannot be captured outside the experience. While testifying to the experience, something this book seeks to do, is a much better mode of witness than reducing the experience to counted dollars and learning outcomes—even then this is but a glimpse of the grace found in this process. Thus, even now, I confess I cannot measure the impact of *Reconciling Practices*. I further confess that this immeasurability is, for me, no indication of lack of value. On the contrary, this cohort has been a testimony to the extravagant, immeasurable grace of God. It is possible to walk together, listen together, and witness together in the deepest of divisions and in the midst of things yet to be resolved and redeemed by the transforming eternal love of God.

> The end of all things is near; therefore be serious and discipline yourselves for the sake of your prayers. Above all, maintain constant love for one another, for love covers a multitude of sins. Be hospitable to one another without complaining. Like good stewards of the manifold grace of God, serve one another with whatever gift each of you has received. Whoever speaks must do so

as one speaking the very words of God; whoever serves must do so with the strength that God supplies, so that God may be glorified in all things through Jesus Christ. To him belong the glory and the power for ever and ever. Amen.

(1 Peter 4:7-11)

CONTRIBUTORS

Cate Anthony
Berkeley Divinity School

Bill Clarkson
Trinity School for Ministry

Emily Collette
Virginia Theological Seminary

Will Dickinson
Berkeley Divinity School

Alice Grant
Anglican Episcopal House of Studies,
Duke Divinity School

Aaron Pelot
Trinity School for Ministry

Peter Schellhase
Nashotah House Theological Seminary

Mason Waldhauser
Nashotah House Theological Seminary

Jill Williams
Virginia Theological Seminary

Travis Wilson
Anglican Episcopal House of Studies,
Duke Divinity School

BIBLIOGRAPHY

Boal, Augusto. *Games for Actors and Non-Actors*, 2nd ed., trans. Adrian Jackson. London and New York: Routledge, 2002.

Heaney, Robert, John Kafwanka K., and Hilda Kabia, eds. *God's Church for God's World: A Practical Approach to Partnership in Mission*. New York: Church Publishing, 2020.

Heaney, Robert S. and William S. Sachs. *The Promise of Anglicanism*. London: SPCK, 2019.

Lambeth Conference. Lambethconference.org/. Accessed December 19, 2020.

Taylor, John V. *The Go-Between God: The Holy Spirit and the Christian Mission*. Eugene: Wipf and Stock, 2015.

Vatican II. "Gaudium et Spes: Pastoral Constitution on the Church in the Modern World." Vatican.va, December 7, 1965. https://www.vatican.va/archive/hist_councils/ii_vatican_council/documents/vat-ii_const_19651207_gaudium-et-spes_en.html.

World Health Organization. https://www.who.int/emergencies/diseases/novel-coronavirus-2019.

FURTHER RESOURCES

BOOKS

Arten, Isaac and William Glass, eds. *A House Divided: Ways Forward for North American Anglicans*. Eugene: Wipf & Stock Publishers, 2015.

Boesak, Allan Aubrey and Curtiss Paul DeYoung. *Radical Reconciliation: Beyond Political Quietism and Christian Quietism*. Maryknoll: Orbis Books, 2012.

Caputo, John D., Mark Dooley, and Michael J. Scanlon, eds. *Questioning God*. Bloomington: Indiana University Press, 2001.

Cone, James. *The Cross and the Lynching Tree*. Maryknoll: Orbis Books, 2015.

Heaney, Robert S. and William S. Sachs. *The Promise of Anglicanism*. London: SCM Press, 2019.

Heaney, Robert S., John Y.H. Yieh, and Jean A. Cotting, eds. *Building Dialogue: Stories, Scripture, and Liturgy in Peacebuilding*. (New York: Morehouse, forthcoming.)

Katongole, Emmanuel. *Born from Lament: The Theology and Politics of Hope in Africa*. Grand Rapids: Wm. B. Eerdmans Publishing Co., 2017.

Kantongle, Emmanuel. *The Journey of Reconciliation: Groaning for New Creation in Africa.* Maryknoll: Orbis Books, 2017.

Kantongle, Emmanuel and Chris Rice. *Reconciling All Things: A Christian Vision of Justice, Peace, and Healing.* Downers Grove: IVP Books, 2008.

Lederach, John Paul. *The Moral Imagination: The Art and Soul of Building Peace.* Oxford: OUP, 2005.

————. *Little Book of Conflict Transformation: Clear Articulation of the Guiding Principles By A Pioneer in the Field.* New York: Good Books, 2003.

Moltmann, Jürgen. *Theology of Hope: On the Ground and Implications of Christian Eschatology*, trans. James W. Leitch and Margaret Kohl. Minneapolis: Fortress Press, 1993.

————. *The Crucified God*, 40th Anniversary Edition. Minneapolis: Fortress Press, 2015.

Poggo, Anthony. *Come Let us Rebuild: Lessons from Nehemiah*, ed. Tim Flatman. Millipede Books, 2013.

Roberts, J. Deotis, *Liberation and Reconciliation: A Black Theology*, 2nd ed. Maryknoll: Orbis Books, 1994.

Swamy, Muthuraj. *Reconciliation: The Archbishop of Canterbury's Lent Book 2019.* London: SPCK, 2018.

Tutu, Desmond Mpilo. *No Future Without Forgiveness.* New York: Doubleday, 1999.

Volf, Miroslav. *Exclusion and Embrace: A Theological Exploration of Identity, Otherness, and Reconciliation.*

Revised and Updated. Nashville: Abingdon Press, 2019.

WEBSITES

Be the Bridge. "BTB101." Bethebridge.com.
https://bethebridge.com/btb101/

Coventry Cathedral. "The Community of the Cross of Nails: Growing Together in Hope." Coventry Cathedral.org.
http://www.coventrycathedral.org. uk/ccn/

"The Coventry Litany of Reconciliation." Coventry Cathedral.org.uk.
http://www.coventrycathedral.org.uk/ccn/the-coventry-litany-of-reconciliation/

Coventry Cathedral. "Resources and Training." CoventryCathedral.org.uk.
http://www.coventrycathedral.org.uk/ccn/resources/.

The Episcopal Church. "Racial Reconciliation." Episcopalchurch.org.
https://www.episcopalchurch.org/ministries/racial-reconciliation/

Global Anglican Future Conference. "The Jerusalem Statement." Gafcon.org. https://www.gafcon.org/about/jerusalem-statement.

Lambeth Commission on Communion. *The Windsor Report*. London: The Anglican Communion Office, 2004. https://www.anglicancommunion.org/media/682 25/windsor2004full.pdf.

"Promotion of National Unity and Reconciliation Act 34 of 1995". Justice.gov.za. https://www.justice.gov.za/legislation/acts/1995-034.pdf.

Rose Castle Foundation. "Marking This Time of Holocaust Memorial." Rosecastle.com. https://www.rosecastle.com/rcf/holocaust-memorial?hsCtaTracking=19f376ae-d59d.

Rose Castle Foundation. "12 Habits of a Reconciler." Rosecastle.com. https://www.rosecastle.com/rcf/habits/downloa d?hsCtaTracking=cb2c7af6-6774-447481de-0a2eb7011376%7C65a3fdb0-3260-4709-a26b-225b2d593b8d.

"St. Michael's House Protocols." Churchofengland. com. https://www.churchofengland.org/sites/default/f iles/2017-12/smh_protocolsjuly2016.pdf.

Virginia Theological Seminary. "Reparations." VTS.edu. https://vts.edu/mission/multiculturalministries/r eparations/.

Virginia Theological Seminary. "Why the Episcopal Church Needs World Anglicanism." YouTube.com. https://www.youtube.com/watch?v=XTHvPHq4E _o.

Virginia Theological Seminary. "2017 Mollegen Forum–'The Vitality of World Anglicanism' with Archbishop Josiah Idowu-Fearon." YouTube.com https://www.youtube.com/watch?v=bFCBz9Knw sQ.